THE 12 MOST INFLUENTIAL
SCIENTIFIC DISCOVERIES
OF ALL TIME

by Emily Rose Oachs

12 STORY LIBRARY

www.12StoryLibrary.com

12-Story Library is an imprint of Bookstaves and Press Room Editions

Produced for 12-Story Library by Red Line Editorial

Photographs ©: choness/iStockphoto, cover, 1; Stefano Bianchetti/Corbis Historical/Getty Images, 4; Rtimages/Shutterstock Images, 5; North Wind Picture Archives, 6; Skylines/Shutterstock Images, 7; Culture Club/Hulton Archive/Getty Images, 8; Marc Ward/Shutterstock Images, 9, 28; Geologist natural pics/Shutterstock Images, 10; Barks/Shutterstock Images, 11; Bettmann/Getty Images, 12, 14; concept w/Shutterstock Images, 13; Yuganov Konstantin/Shutterstock Images, 15; Everett Historical/Shutterstock Images, 16, 20; EricVega/iStockphoto, 17; Albert Edelfelt/North Wind Picture Archives, 18; Baloncici/Shutterstock Images, 19; Maurizio De Mattei/Shutterstock Images, 21; vitstudio/Shutterstock Images, 22, 29; isak55/Shutterstock Images, 23; Juan Gaertner/Shutterstock Images, 24; anyaivanova/Shutterstock Images, 25; Alex Tihonovs/Shutterstock Images, 26; Johnrob/iStockphoto, 27

Library of Congress Cataloging-in-Publication Data
Names: Oachs, Emily Rose.
Title: The 12 most influential scientific discoveries of all time / by Emily
    Rose Oachs.
Description: Mankato, MN : 12 Story Library, [2018] | Series: The most
    influential | Audience: Grade 4 to 6. | Includes bibliographical
    references and index.
Identifiers: LCCN 2016047131 (print) | LCCN 2016048615 (ebook) | ISBN
    9781632354136 (hardcover : alk. paper) | ISBN 9781632354846 (pbk. : alk.
    paper) | ISBN 9781621435365 (hosted e-book)
Subjects: LCSH: Discoveries in science—History—Juvenile literature. |
    Science—History—Juvenile literature.
Classification: LCC Q180.55.D57 O23 2018 (print) | LCC Q180.55.D57 (ebook) |
    DDC 509—dc23
LC record available at https://lccn.loc.gov/2016047131

Printed in the United States of America
022017

Access free, up-to-date content on this topic plus a full digital version of this book. Scan the QR code on page 31 or use your school's login at 12StoryLibrary.com.

Table of Contents

The Earth Is Round 4

The Copernican Model Opens Up the Universe 6

Gravity Leads to Modern Physics 8

Fossils Reveal the Past 10

Oxygen Makes Way for Chemistry 12

Vaccines Keep People Healthy 14

Electricity Powers Modern Life 16

Pasteurization Kills Bacteria 18

Evolution Changes the World of Science 20

DNA Unlocks the Mystery of Genes 22

Stem Cells Transform Medicine 24

Climate Change Alters Habits 26

Other Notable Scientific Discoveries 28

Glossary 30

For More Information 31

Index 32

About the Author 32

1

The Earth Is Round

Many ancient people believed Earth was flat. They imagined Earth as a disk sitting in the middle of an ocean. Others thought Earth was shaped like a cube. An ancient Greek scholar named Pythagoras had a different idea. He knew the moon and sun were spheres. In approximately 500 BCE, he suggested Earth was a sphere, too.

Scientists continued to build on this idea. A scholar named Eratosthenes was interested in measuring Earth's sphere in approximately 245 BCE. To do this, he looked at the angle of the sun's rays as they hit Earth. He used the measurements to estimate Earth's size. It was the first time anyone had tried to do this.

Many centuries later, people first traveled around the whole globe. In 1519 CE, an explorer named Ferdinand Magellan set sail from Spain. He traveled west across

Ferdinand Magellan led the expedition that was the first to travel around the globe.

24,898
Approximate distance, in miles (40,069 km), around Earth at the equator.

- Many ancient people believed Earth was flat.
- Around 500 BCE the ancient Greeks suggested Earth was not flat.
- Ferdinand Magellan's expedition was the first to travel around the globe.

THINK ABOUT IT

What clues helped the ancient Greeks conclude that Earth is round? What other proof exists today? Find articles and look up these topics online to learn more.

From there, the ships continued sailing west until they reached Spain again. This trip gave people a more accurate idea of Earth's size.

the Atlantic Ocean. When his ships reached the bottom of South America, they sailed through a strait. It led to the Pacific Ocean.

Learning about Earth's size and shape allowed people to make more accurate maps.

The Copernican Model Opens Up the Universe

For centuries, people believed that Earth did not move. They thought it stood at the center of the universe. They also believed the sun, stars, and other planets all circled Earth.

In 1543, an astronomer named Nicolaus Copernicus published a book with a different idea. He had been studying the night sky in Italy. Copernicus thought that Earth and the other planets circled the sun.

Studying the night sky inspired Copernicus's idea of planets revolving around the sun.

92.6 million

Approximate distance, in miles (149,600,000 km), between Earth and the sun.

- Until Copernicus, most people believed Earth stayed in place and the universe orbited around it.
- Copernicus argued that Earth and the planets circle the sun.
- The Copernican model brought a deeper understanding of the universe.

The Copernican model helped explain day and night.

He believed that while Earth was orbiting, it was also rotating on its axis. His idea became known as the Copernican model. Within a century, most people had accepted it.

The Copernican model helped explain how time passes. It takes Earth approximately 365 days to complete one orbit around the sun. This time is marked as one year. Earth takes 24 hours to rotate on its axis one time. This is the length of one day.

In 1609, astronomer Johannes Kepler built on the Copernican model. Copernicus had believed the

GALILEO GALILEI

Galileo Galilei was an astronomer in the 1600s. He believed in the Copernican model. In 1633, the Catholic Church put Galileo on trial. It claimed he was going against the Church by believing Copernicus. The Church believed the Bible clearly showed that the sun circles Earth. Galileo lost the trial. He was locked up in his home for the rest of his life.

planets orbited in a path shaped like a circle. Kepler disagreed. He thought they orbited the sun in a path shaped like an oval. Many later scientists have based their studies on Kepler's model. With it, they have discovered even more about how the universe works.

Gravity Leads to Modern Physics

Isaac Newton was a student in the 1660s. One day, he saw an apple fall to the ground. Newton began to wonder why objects always fall straight down. Soon, he started to study the force that pulled objects to the ground.

In time, Newton understood that this force stretched beyond Earth. He realized the force that made apples fall also made the planets orbit the sun. Newton named that force gravity.

In 1687, Newton published *Principia Mathematica*. In it, he explained his findings about gravity. Through gravity, objects are attracted toward each other.

As the understanding of gravity grew, a new branch of science called physics began. Scientists used gravity to explain many events in the universe. Planets are matter held together by gravity. Gravity is the force that makes Earth orbit the sun. Gravity traps water and gases on Earth. Without them, no life could survive on Earth.

Watching an apple fall from a tree inspired Newton's study of gravity.

THINK ABOUT IT

What is gravity like on other planets? On the moon? Look this up online to find out more.

25,000

Miles per hour (40,233 km/h) an object must travel to escape Earth's gravity.

- In 1687, Isaac Newton published his ideas about gravity.
- Newton realized the same force controls falling objects and orbiting planets.
- Modern sciences came from Newton's discovery.

Later scientists studied the effects of gravity in space. Astronauts appear weightless in space. That's because gravity in space is weaker than on Earth. The astronauts are still falling toward Earth, but at a slower rate. At the same time, the astronauts are orbiting Earth at a very high speed. The result is that they appear to float.

Today, astronauts study the effects of weaker gravity on human bodies, plants, and animals. Scientist also use gravity to keep space stations and satellites from floating away into space.

The International Space Station relies on gravity to stay in place.

Fossils Reveal the Past

Fossils are the hardened remains of plants and animals. A few ancient scientists understood this. Most people did not. Some believed fossils had special powers. Others thought they had grown inside rocks. In China, people thought dinosaur fossils were dragon bones.

In the 1500s, Leonardo da Vinci suggested fossils were remains of living things. During the 1700s, this understanding of fossils became common. Soon, people began to collect and study fossils.

In 1793, English engineer William Smith made an important discovery about fossils. Smith realized that some fossils only appeared in specific layers of Earth's crust. The fossils and the layers in which they were found provided clues to Earth's history. From them, scientists could figure out how Earth's climate and land had changed over thousands of years.

The discovery of fossils also led to paleontology. It is the science of plants and animals that lived in prehistoric times. Fossils reveal what an animal ate and where it lived. They also show how some animals may have changed over time.

Fossils must be dug from the earth carefully.

3.5 billion
Age in years of the oldest known fossil.

- Ancient people believed fossils grew inside rocks or held special powers.
- In the 1700s, people began to collect and study fossils.
- Fossils allow people to learn about past plants, animals, and peoples.

GREATEST FOSSILIST

Mary Anning was a British fossil collector in the 1800s who made important discoveries. When she was a child, she and her brother found the first bones from an ichthyosaurus. Later, she uncovered the skeletons of other prehistoric creatures. Today, Anning is known as "the greatest fossilist the world ever knew."

For many years, paleontologists used basic tools, such as microscopes. Today, these tools are much more powerful. Electron microscopes allow scientists to see a fossil's tiniest details. CT scans show the structures inside fossils. Computer programs use fossils to reconstruct how an animal may have looked and moved. These tools have given people a clearer picture of Earth's past.

Dinosaur fossils, such as this triceratops, can be reassembled to show how they looked.

Oxygen Makes Way for Chemistry

Modern scientists know that Earth has 118 elements, such as oxygen, carbon, and iron. Early scientists viewed the world differently. They believed Earth was made of four main elements. They were earth, air, fire, and water. In the 1700s, people began to look at the world in a new, scientific way.

One of the scientists working during this time was Carl Scheele of Sweden. Around 1772, Scheele became the first person to isolate oxygen. He did not publish his discovery until 1777. In the meantime, English scientist Joseph Priestley had also discovered oxygen in 1774. The discoveries made by

19
Average amount, in cubic feet (.5 cubic m), of oxygen a person uses each day.

- Oxygen was first discovered in the 1770s.
- It led to a better understanding of fire and breathing.
- Its discovery resulted in the creation of the science called chemistry.

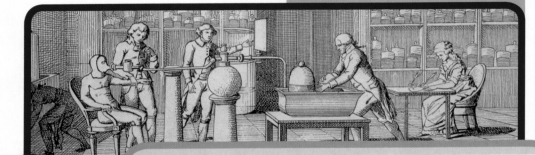

Antoine-Laurent Lavoisier conducted many experiments on breathing and oxygen in his laboratory.

PERIODIC TABLE OF THE ELEMENTS

Earth's elements are organized in a chart called the Periodic Table of the Elements.

Scheele and Priestley became well known among scientists in Europe.

French scientist Antoine-Laurent Lavoisier built on the work of Scheele and Priestley. He gave oxygen its name. In his experiments, Lavoisier realized that air is made up of multiple elements. Oxygen is just one part of air. Lavoisier also explained the role of oxygen in breathing and in burning.

Later, scientists learned that when oxygen combines with other elements, new substances are formed. For example, when hydrogen and oxygen combine, they form water. Scientists also learned the role of plants in the creation of oxygen. That process is known as photosynthesis.

The discovery of oxygen also brought about a new kind of science called chemistry. It is the study of the elements that make up the universe. Today, chemists work in many fields. Some study living creatures. Others study nonliving things, such as rocks and metals. Chemists also work with food products, chemicals, plastics, and even medicines.

Vaccines Keep People Healthy

In the 1700s, Edward Jenner was a doctor in England. At the time, smallpox killed 400,000 people each year in Europe. About one-third of people who recovered became blind. Most survivors had terrible scars. Jenner had heard stories about women who never seemed to get the disease. These milkmaids had all caught cowpox previously. It was a disease like smallpox but much milder. Jenner believed having cowpox had made the women immune.

Jenner tested his idea in 1796. He rubbed part of a cowpox blister on a boy's arm. The boy became ill

Edward Jenner tested his vaccine on eight-year-old James Phipps.

Vaccines have saved the lives of millions of children.

for a few days. But soon, he felt better. Months later, Jenner tried to infect the boy with smallpox. The boy did not become sick. Jenner's experiment was a success. It led to the creation of vaccines. They help to stop infectious diseases.

Soon, other doctors started to vaccinate their patients against smallpox. Far fewer people caught the disease. The number of deaths from smallpox went down.

Other diseases now have their own vaccines. Polio, mumps, tetanus, and measles are just a few examples. With vaccinations, these diseases have become much less common. Most children are

vaccinated beginning from birth. This keeps communities safe and healthy. Scientists continue to develop many new vaccines. They hope to end diseases such as malaria, AIDS, and tuberculosis.

1979
Year smallpox was officially eradicated.

- Edward Jenner first vaccinated a child against smallpox in 1796.
- Vaccinations can provide immunity to certain diseases.
- Polio, rabies, and measles have their own vaccines.

15

Electricity Powers Modern Life

In 1752, Benjamin Franklin performed an experiment with lightning. He attached a key to a kite. Lightning struck a metal pole in the kite and traveled to the key. It created a spark. Franklin's experiment proved that lightning was electricity, although he was lucky he didn't die.

A huge step forward in harnessing the power of electricity came in 1831. Michael Faraday realized that magnets could pass electricity through wires. This discovery led to the invention of the electrical

Franklin's experiment with lightning brought a greater understanding of electricity.

1.3 billion

Estimated number of people around the world who have electricity.

- In 1752, Benjamin Franklin learned that lightning is electricity.
- Thomas Edison began building power stations in the late 1800s.
- Electricity is a part of everyday life for many people.

16

generator. It helped make it possible for electricity to be mass produced.

Thomas Edison invented an affordable lightbulb in 1879. Soon after, he began to build power plants. Underground wires carried electricity from the plants into buildings. For the first time, people had electricity in their homes.

Electricity changed how many people lived. People no longer relied on candles, gas lamps, and fireplaces for light and heat. Instead, they could use electric lights and furnaces. In the summer, electric air conditioners cooled homes. Electricity also powered dishwashers, refrigerators, televisions, and other appliances.

THE POWER OF NIAGARA FALLS

Niagara Falls separates the United States from Canada. It is made up of three huge waterfalls. In the 1890s, people saw the natural power of the falls. They wanted to use Niagara Falls to create electricity. People began to build power plants on the falls. Today, Niagara Falls produces enough electricity to power 3.8 million homes.

Homes wired for electricity changed how people lived.

Pasteurization Kills Bacteria

In the 1850s, Louis Pasteur was a scientist in France. He was studying alcohol. He wanted to find out what made it spoil. Soon, Pasteur realized that bacteria were making it go bad. He knew that heat could kill those bacteria.

In 1862, Pasteur created a heating and cooling process for liquids.

The heat would kill all the bacteria. It would make the liquid safe to drink. Yet it would not destroy the natural flavor. This process became known as pasteurization. It was used on beer, wine, and vinegar.

In 1882, the first equipment to pasteurize milk became available.

Louis Pasteur

30 minutes

Length of time milk must be heated to 145°F (63°C) before it is considered pasteurized.

- In 1862, Louis Pasteur created a process to kill harmful bacteria in drinks.
- Pasteurization prevents the spread of deadly diseases through food and drinks.
- Most dairy products are pasteurized today.

A large tank at a dairy factory heats milk to pasteurize it, making it safe to drink.

Before this time, sometimes milk contained dangerous bacteria. It could make people vomit and could even lead to death. By pasteurizing milk, people could drink it without fear. Today, milk, cheese, yogurt, and other dairy products are usually pasteurized.

Pasteurization lengthens the shelf life of foods and drinks. It keeps foods safe from spoiling quickly. In addition to milk, commonly pasteurized foods are eggs, almonds, and fruit juice. The process kills much of the bacteria in those foods. It keeps these foods from spreading deadly diseases, such as Salmonella, E. coli, and Listeria. Pasteurization has saved millions of lives.

Evolution Changes the World of Science

9

In 1831, English scientist Charles Darwin took a trip that would change science forever. That December, Darwin set sail on the *HMS Beagle.* Over the next five years, he studied animals on four continents. This trip inspired his theory of evolution. He spent many years studying, thinking, and writing about it.

In 1859, Darwin published a book about his theory. It was called *On the Origin of Species.* In it, Darwin wrote that all living things share a common ancestor. He explained that animals with certain traits are

Charles Darwin's theories furthered the understanding of life on Earth.

1,250
Number of first-edition copies published of *On the Origin of Species.*

- Charles Darwin published his theory of evolution in 1859.
- Darwin's theory of evolution laid the foundation for more study.
- It changed people's understanding of how life began.

more likely to survive. These traits make the animals better suited to their surroundings. The animals then pass these traits on to their children. In time, these animals could change into a new species. This was his theory of evolution.

Darwin's book was an instant success. The first edition sold out immediately. Soon, most scientists accepted Darwin's theory of evolution. Scientists built upon it as they learned more. Over the years, it has changed a great deal.

Darwin's theory brought a better understanding of nature. It gave people a scientific way to think about life. In the past, many people turned to religion to explain the world around them. Most people at the time believed Earth had existed for only approximately 6,000 years. Evolution helped show that Earth has been around for much longer. It also showed people how life came to be.

THE WALKING WHALE

Darwin used whales as an example of evolution in his book. He suggested that whales may have evolved from a land animal. In 1994, scientists discovered a fossil from an ancestor of the whale. The *Ambulocetus natans* was a "walking" whale. It lived 49 million years ago. It could swim in water and walk on land.

Darwin studied finches from the Galapagos Islands to better understand evolution.

DNA Unlocks the Mystery of Genes

Every living being has DNA. It holds the instructions for each cell. DNA determines a person's hair color, eye color, and height. It can also determine if a person gets some diseases or disorders. How people got these traits was a mystery for many years.

Then in 1869, a Swiss doctor named Friedrich Miescher made a discovery. He was studying cells. He discovered a new substance in cells and called it *nuclein*. Today, it is known as DNA. At the time of Miescher's discovery, scientists did not understand DNA's importance. In the 1940s, scientists made a big discovery. They found that DNA passed traits from parents to children.

English scientist Rosalind Franklin used a method called X-ray diffraction to study DNA. It allowed

The double helix shape of DNA looks like two spirals twisted together.

THE HUMAN GENOME PROJECT

In 1990, the Human Genome Project started. Scientists wanted to find all the genes that make up a person's DNA. They accomplished this in 2003. Now, scientists can better spot possible diseases that a person's DNA carries. They can also find differences between the DNA of humans and other organisms.

her to learn more about what makes up DNA and its spiral shape. James Watson and Francis Crick used Franklin's findings. In 1953, they discovered that DNA is actually two spirals. This shape is called a double helix. The structure helped scientists understand how DNA traits were passed down.

The discovery of DNA has affected many parts of life. Today, people can test their DNA to see if they carry genes for diseases. At crime scenes, detectives collect DNA samples. Then, they can match these samples to possible criminals. With DNA, scientists can also copy cells and genes.

20,500
Estimated number of genes made by DNA in a human body.

- DNA was first found in 1869.
- In 1944, scientists discovered that DNA carries an organism's traits.
- DNA lets scientists clone and run tests for certain diseases.

Scientists can map DNA to discover if a person has inherited a disease.

Father/Child

Sizing Mark

Mother

Father

Stem Cells Transform Medicine

Stem cells are a special type of human cell. They have the ability to form any body part. Stem cells could become a liver, a kidney, or even a brain. Embryos are one source of stem cells. The small intestine, brain, and spinal cord are sources of stem cells, too. They are also in bone marrow, which is the tissue inside a bone.

In 1957, Dr. E. Donnall Thomas of New York performed the first successful stem cell therapy. He was treating a patient with cancer. Thomas killed the patient's cancer cells with radiation. Then he removed bone marrow from a healthy person. He gave it to the cancer patient. It helped the patient regrow healthy cells to replace those that the radiation had destroyed.

Before the work of Thomas, many types of cancer were not curable. Bone marrow transplants

Stem cells can improve the treatment for many diseases.

Using stem cells is a new field in science.

greatly increased the chances of surviving many types of cancer. For his work, Thomas received the Nobel Prize in medicine.

Today, scientists know more about stem cells. Stem cells have the potential to heal many diseases. They can also provide clues about how human cells divide and grow into organs. In the future, stem cells may regrow organs, restore sight, and cure diabetes. Stem cells have the potential to improve the health of people across the globe.

200

Approximate number of different types of cells a human body has.

- Stem cells have the potential to become any body part.
- The small intestine, brain, spinal cord, bone marrow, and embryos are some of the sources of stem cells.
- Doctors use stem cells to cure certain types of cancer.

Climate Change Alters Habits

In 1896, Svante Arrhenius suggested humans could change Earth's climate. The Swiss scientist believed that burning fossil fuels would make Earth warmer. He was the first to suggest this idea. The theory gained proof in 1938. That year, data showed the planet's temperature was rising.

Soon, scientists were studying the world's climate. They discovered that burning fossil fuels creates a gas called carbon dioxide. It traps heat inside Earth's atmosphere. The result is warmer temperatures across the globe.

In 1988, scientists from around the world joined together. They planned to study climate change. In 2013, the group announced that Earth's average temperature had risen since 1880. It was 1.5 degrees Fahrenheit (0.9°C) warmer. Human actions have caused most of the increase.

Exhaust from power plants, factories, and incinerators are major sources of pollution that cause global warming.

8.6

Number of degrees, in Fahrenheit (4.8°C), Earth's temperature is expected to rise between 2005 and 2100.

- Scientists found that burning fossil fuels makes Earth warmer.
- By 2013, Earth's average temperature had risen by 1.5 degrees Fahrenheit (0.9°C) since 1880.
- People are changing their habits to produce less greenhouse gases.

THINK ABOUT IT

A carbon footprint is the amount of carbon dioxide a person emits into the atmosphere. How can you reduce the carbon footprint of your home or school?

Many cities now offer bicycles for rent as an alternative to driving.

The group also warned that the warming could continue.

Today, people worry about the effects of climate change. Warmer weather melts Earth's glaciers. As a result, sea levels rise and can cause flooding. Climate change also affects weather patterns. Some areas may get too much rain, while others may not get enough. Plants bloom earlier and animals move to cooler areas.

Reversing climate change will take a long time. Many people want to do their part to help. They make small changes to their everyday habits.

They choose not to burn fossil fuels by driving. Instead, they bike or take public transportation. Other people try to recycle, use less electricity, and plant trees. They hope these actions will help to slow climate change.

27

Other Notable Scientific Discoveries

Birds Belong to a Family of Dinosaurs

For many years, scientists believed birds were the only animals to have feathers. That idea changed in the 1990s. At that time, scientists found new dinosaur fossils in China. The fossils had an early type of bristle-like feathers. From this evidence, scientists began to realize that birds are related to dinosaurs. Scientists believe birds descend from a dinosaur family called therapods. It includes dinosaurs such as the Tyrannosaurus rex.

Bacteria Cause Ulcers

Ulcers are painful sores often found in the stomach. In the past, doctors thought ulcers were caused by stress. They believed ulcers could not be an infection. Doctors thought acids in the stomach would kill any bacteria that could cause an infection.

Two Australian scientists, Barry J. Marshall and J. Robin Warren, proved this idea wrong. They showed that a type of bacteria called *Helicobacter pylori* can grow in the stomach and create ulcers. This discovery changed how ulcers are treated. Instead of suffering for years, patients can take antibiotics and recover quickly. In 2005, Marshall and Warren won the Nobel Prize for medicine for this work.

Vitamin C Cures Scurvy

For many years, people did not realize the link between food and health. One of the oldest illnesses people suffered from was scurvy. People with scurvy had bleeding gums, loose teeth that often fell out, stiff joints, and bleeding under the skin. No one knew how to cure scurvy or what caused it. In 1753, a Scottish doctor named James Lind discovered that eating foods high in vitamin C could prevent and cure scurvy. Eating oranges and limes became the prescription for scurvy. This once-common disease could be cured easily thanks to Lind.

Glossary

ancestor
A relative who lived long ago.

blister
A bubble in the skin that is filled with liquid.

embryo
An unborn human or animal that is in the early stages of developing.

fossil fuel
A type of fuel created from plants and animals that died long ago.

generator
A machine that produces electricity.

infectious
Able to be passed from one person to another.

isolate
To separate.

species
A group of living things that all share some qualities.

sphere
A shape that is round, like a ball.

trait
A feature or characteristic that sets something apart.

For More Information

Books

Demuth, Patricia Brennan. *Who Was Galileo?* New York: Grosset & Dunlap, 2015.

Goldsmith, Mike. *Eureka! The Most Amazing Scientific Discoveries of All Time.* New York: Thames & Hudson, 2014.

Wood, Susan. *Vaccine Innovators Pearl Kendrick and Grace Eldering.* Minneapolis: Lerner Publications, 2017.

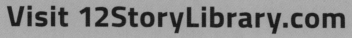

Visit 12StoryLibrary.com

Scan the code or use your school's login at **12StoryLibrary.com** for recent updates about this topic and a full digital version of this book. Enjoy free access to:

- Digital ebook
- Breaking news updates
- Live content feeds
- Videos, interactive maps, and graphics
- Additional web resources

Note to educators: Visit 12StoryLibrary.com/register to sign up for free premium website access. Enjoy live content plus a full digital version of every 12-Story Library book you own for every student at your school.

Editor's note: The 12 topics featured in this book are selected by the author and approved by the book's editor. While not a definitive list, the selected topics are an attempt to balance the book's subject with the intended readership. To expand learning about this subject, please visit **12StoryLibrary.com** or use this book's QR code to access free additional content.

Index

Anning, Mary, 11
Arrhenius, Svante, 26

cancer, 24–25
chemistry, 13
climate change, 26–27
Copernican Model, 7
Copernicus, Nicolaus,
   6–7

Darwin, Charles, 20–21
da Vinci, Leonardo, 10
DNA, 22–23

Edison, Thomas, 17
electricity, 16–17, 27
Eratosthenes, 4
evolution, 20–21

fossil fuels, 26–27
fossils, 10–11, 21

Franklin, Benjamin, 16
Franklin, Rosalind,
   22–23

Galilei, Galileo, 7
genes, 22–23
gravity, 8–9

Human Genome Project,
   22

Jenner, Edward, 14–15

Kepler, Johannes, 7

Lavoisier, Antoine-
   Laurent, 13
lightbulb, 17

Miescher, Freidrich, 22

Niagara Falls, 17
Newton, Isaac, 8
Nobel Prize, 25, 29

On the Origin of Species,
   20
oxygen, 12–13

paleontology, 10–11
Pasteur, Louis, 18
pasteurization, 18–19
physics, 8
Priestley, Joseph, 12–13
Principia Mathematica, 8
Pythagoras, 4

Scheele, Carl, 12–13
smallpox, 14–15
Smith, William, 10
stem cells, 24–25

Thomas, E. Donnall,
   24–25

vaccines, 15

About the Author

Emily Rose Oachs graduated from the University of Minnesota. She has authored more than 50 nonfiction books for children and young adults, on topics ranging from natural disasters and biomes to geography and history. She lives and writes in Los Angeles, California.

32